SPORTS' WILDEST UPSETS

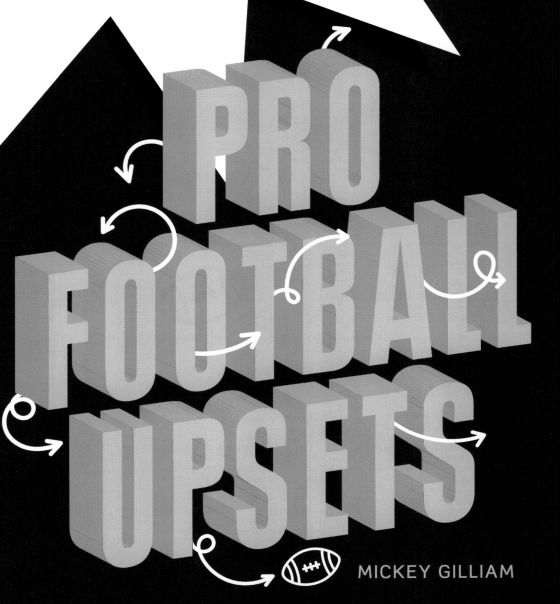

PRO FOOTBALL UPSETS

MICKEY GILLIAM

Lerner Publications ◆ Minneapolis

Copyright © 2020 by Lerner Publishing Group, Inc.

All rights reserved. International copyright secured. No part of this book may be reproduced, stored in a retrieval system, or transmitted in any form or by any means—electronic, mechanical, photocopying, recording, or otherwise—without the prior written permission of Lerner Publishing Group, Inc., except for the inclusion of brief quotations in an acknowledged review.

Lerner Publications Company
An imprint of Lerner Publishing Group, Inc.
241 First Avenue North
Minneapolis, MN 55401 USA

For reading levels and more information, look up this title at www.lernerbooks.com.

Main body text set in Aptifer Sans LT Pro.
Typeface provided by Linotype AG.

Library of Congress Cataloging-in-Publication Data

Names: Gilliam, Mickey author. | Lerner Publishing Group, Inc.
Title: Pro football upsets / Mickey Gilliam.
Description: Minneapolis : Lerner Publications, [2020] | Series: Sports' wildest upsets (Lerner Sports) | Audience: Ages: 7–11. | Audience: Grades: 4 to 6. | Includes bibliographical references and index.
Identifiers: LCCN 2019016682 (print) | LCCN 2019021885 (ebook) | ISBN 9781541583696 (eb pdf) | ISBN 9781541577091 (library binding : alk. paper) | ISBN 9781541589674 (paperback : alk. paper)
Subjects: LCSH: National Football League—History—Juvenile literature. | Sports upsets—United States—History—Juvenile literature. | National Football League—Miscellanea—Juvenile literature. | Football—United States—History—Juvenile literature. | Sports rivalries—United States—History—Juvenile literature.
Classification: LCC GV955.5.N35 (ebook) | LCC GV955.5.N35 G57 2020 (print) | DDC 796.332/640973—dc23

LC record available at https://lccn.loc.gov/2019016682

Manufactured in the United States of America
1 – CG – 12/31/19

CONTENTS

Upsets can happen anytime during the NFL season.

OPENING KICKOFF

FOOTBALL IS THE MOST POPULAR PROFESSIONAL SPORT IN THE UNITED STATES. The talent, hard work, and rivalries are what have kept people interested over the years. Fans compare the 32 teams in the National Football League (NFL) and enjoy arguing over which team is best. They root for their favorites to reach the Super Bowl at the end of the season.

The greatest upsets in the NFL often come during the playoffs. The playoff teams with the best regular-season records play those with the worst. But every squad in the playoffs is a good one. That means they can beat anyone if they perform well enough. The amount of talent in the league also means that any team, no matter how bad the team's season, has the ability to rise to the top and win.

FACTS AT A GLANCE

- In the 1950 season opener, the Cleveland Browns beat the defending champion Philadelphia Eagles. It was Cleveland's first game in the NFL. However, Cleveland had previously played in a different league called the All-America Football Conference.

- The New York Jets upset the Baltimore Colts on January 12, 1969. It was the first time a team from the American Football League (AFL) defeated an NFL team in the Super Bowl.

- The 1996 Jacksonville Jaguars made the playoffs in their second year of existence. They pulled off an epic upset, beating the Denver Broncos in the playoffs.

- The New England Patriots would have had a perfect season if they had won Super Bowl XLII. Instead, the New York Giants beat the odds and defeated the Patriots.

UNBEATEN NO LONGER

THE PLAYERS FROM THE 1972 MIAMI DOLPHINS WERE NERVOUS ON FEBRUARY 3, 2008. They were the only team in modern NFL history to go undefeated. The 1972 Dolphins won all 17 games they played, including the Super Bowl. They wanted to remain the only team to do so.

The New York Giants faced the New England Patriots at Super Bowl XLII.

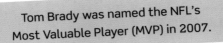

Tom Brady was named the NFL's Most Valuable Player (MVP) in 2007.

The New England Patriots had not lost a game that season. Most people believed they would win the championship game against the New York Giants. Then the 2007 Patriots would join the 1972 Dolphins as the only two teams with a perfect season.

The Patriots were loaded with talent. Best of all was quarterback Tom Brady. He had thrown for nearly 5,000 yards that season. He had also set an NFL record that year with 50 touchdown passes. Nearly half those scores landed in the arms of Randy Moss. Moss was one of the best wide receivers in football history.

David Tyree's helmet catch is considered one of the greatest catches in the history of the Super Bowl.

The game remained close throughout. Both defenses dominated the first three quarters. Quarterback Eli Manning put the Giants ahead on a touchdown pass to David Tyree. Brady answered with a scoring strike to Moss.

One minute remained in the game. The Giants trailed by four. Manning escaped a fierce New England rush. He bolted to the right and fired a long pass. Tyree leaped and pinned the ball between his hand and helmet. It was an incredible catch.

Plaxico Burress celebrated after his game-winning touchdown.

With just 39 seconds left, Giants wide receiver Plaxico Burress sprinted past Patriots cornerback Ellis Hobbs. Manning lofted an arcing pass. Burress snagged it for the go-ahead touchdown.

The Patriots had blown their perfect season. And the 1972 Dolphins were very happy about it.

THAT'S A LOT OF RINGS

Tom Brady has the most Super Bowl rings of any player in NFL history. He has played in nine Super Bowls and won six.

FINAL SCORE

GIANTS **17** | PATRIOTS **14**

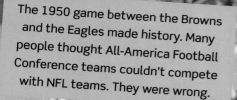

The 1950 game between the Browns and the Eagles made history. Many people thought All-America Football Conference teams couldn't compete with NFL teams. They were wrong.

THE NEW TEAM IN TOWN

THE PHILADELPHIA EAGLES WERE SUPPOSED TO DESTROY THE CLEVELAND BROWNS IN THE 1950 SEASON OPENER. The Eagles had won the 1949 NFL title. The Browns had dominated the All-America Football Conference. But that **disbanded** league was weaker than the NFL. Most believed the Eagles would clobber Cleveland in the Browns' first NFL game.

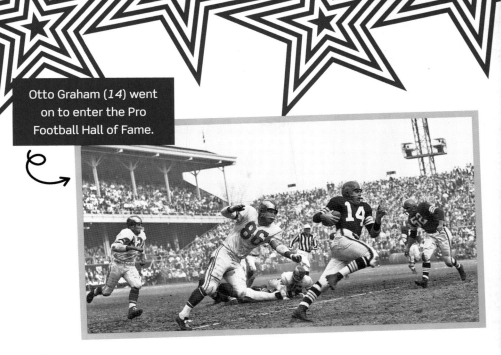

Otto Graham (*14*) went on to enter the Pro Football Hall of Fame.

But the Browns came out quick. Super Cleveland quarterback Otto Graham fired passes all over the field. The trio of Dub Jones, Mac Speedie, and Dante Lavelli sprinted past Eagles defenders. They combined for 16 catches, 355 total yards, and three scores in a big Browns victory.

The Browns proved they were for real. And soon they proved they were the best team in any football league. They went on to win the 1950 NFL championship.

FINAL SCORE

BROWNS	EAGLES
35	**10**

THE BROWNS WERE THE BEST

The Browns went on to be the most successful NFL team of the 1950s. They played in every title game but one from 1950 to 1957. Cleveland won three NFL championships during that stretch.

BATTERED OILERS BEAT CHARGERS

THE SAN DIEGO CHARGERS THOUGHT THEY HAD CAUGHT A BREAK IN THE 1979 PLAYOFFS. Their first opponent, the Houston Oilers, had lost some of their best players to injuries, such as starting quarterback Dan Pastorini and running back Earl Campbell. Without their top offensive players, Houston was a huge **underdog**.

The San Diego Chargers and quarterback Dan Fouts (14) were expected to handle the Houston Oilers in the 1979 playoffs.

Replacement quarterback Gifford Nielsen (*left*) led the Houston Oilers to a win on December 29, 1979.

San Diego scored on its first possession, driving 81 yards down the field. But Oilers defensive back Vernon Perry had a breakout game. He intercepted two passes and blocked a field goal attempt before the half. Houston was able to take the lead at halftime.

The Chargers weren't going down without a fight. They scored again on their first possession of the third quarter. But Houston quarterback Gifford Nielsen responded with a touchdown pass to Mike Renfro. Two more **interceptions** by Perry sealed the deal. The Oilers came away with an incredible victory.

FINAL SCORE

OILERS **17** | CHARGERS **14**

The Denver Broncos were 13–3 at the end of the 1996 season. Most expected them to crush the Jaguars in the playoffs.

UNDERDOGS AT MILE HIGH STADIUM

FEW BELIEVED THE JACKSONVILLE JAGUARS WOULD EVEN MAKE THE PLAYOFFS IN 1996. After all, they were only in their second year of existence. But there they were, playing against future Hall of Fame quarterback John Elway and a dynamite Denver Broncos defense.

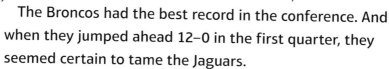

The Broncos had the best record in the conference. And when they jumped ahead 12–0 in the first quarter, they seemed certain to tame the Jaguars.

But Jacksonville quarterback Mark Brunell and running back Natrone Means had other ideas. Means broke two tackles and ran outside for a touchdown. Kicker Mike Hollis nailed two field goals. He put up another in the second half. Jacksonville took charge.

Brunell drove his team down the field, securing a 10-point lead on a touchdown pass to wide receiver Jimmy Smith. The Broncos were able to score once more, but in the end, it wasn't enough to make a comeback.

FINAL SCORE

JAGUARS | BRONCOS
30 | **27**

Mark Brunell played for the Green Bay Packers before being traded to the Jacksonville Jaguars. He went on to set many records for the Jaguars.

HAIL TO THE CHIEFS

MOST PEOPLE WERE CONVINCED THAT THE NFL CHAMPION MINNESOTA VIKINGS WOULD WIPE OUT THE AFL WINNER KANSAS CITY CHIEFS IN THE SUPER BOWL ON JANUARY 11, 1970. The Vikings had scored the most points in the league that season. The Chiefs had only scored 36 points in their last three games combined.

Jim Lynch of the Kansas City Chiefs lent a helping hand to Minnesota Vikings quarterback Joe Kapp during Super Bowl IV.

Otis Taylor's 46-yard touchdown catch sealed the win for Kansas City.

Kansas City forged ahead 16–0 on three field goals and a touchdown run by Mike Garrett. Minnesota tried to battle back with a touchdown in the third quarter.

Soon speedy Chiefs receiver Otis Taylor clinched the victory. He snagged a short pass from quarterback Len Dawson. He then broke a tackle and dashed into the end zone. The Chiefs also intercepted three passes and recovered two **fumbles** in the game.

There was a wipeout on Super Bowl Sunday. But it was the Chiefs wiping out the Vikings.

FINAL SCORE

CHIEFS 23 | VIKINGS 7

Johnny Unitas was one of the greatest quarterbacks of all time.

THE SURPRISING SHUTOUT

THE 1964 BALTIMORE COLTS HAD ONE OF THE GREATEST QUARTERBACKS EVER IN JOHNNY UNITAS. Their lineup also included running back Lenny Moore and receiver Raymond Berry, both future Hall of Famers.

The Colts were expecting an easy championship win. They just needed to stop Cleveland Browns super back Jim Brown from running wild. Brown made a few big plays. But he was not the star of the game that day.

Instead, Cleveland quarterback Frank Ryan and wide receiver Gary Collins took over. The two combined for three touchdowns after a scoreless first half.

Cleveland running back Jim Brown took on a crowd of Baltimore Colts defenders.

Most surprising was Cleveland's defense. The Browns gave up more yards than any defense in the NFL that year. But they shut down the powerful Colts that day.

The Browns pulled off a stunning victory. Their fans celebrated by rushing onto the field and tearing down the goalposts.

FINAL SCORE

BROWNS | COLTS
27 | 0

19

CARTER CATCHES LIKE CRAZY

THE MINNESOTA VIKINGS HAD SURPRISED THE NEW ORLEANS SAINTS IN THE 1987 NATIONAL FOOTBALL CONFERENCE (NFC) WILD-CARD GAME. But a playoff showdown at San Francisco against the 49ers was expected to end their season.

The San Francisco 49ers were a huge favorite with only two losses all season, while the Minnesota Vikings crawled into the playoffs with an 8–7 record.

The 49ers had won 13 games that year. And they had two of the greatest NFL players of all time in quarterback Joe Montana and wide receiver Jerry Rice. The Vikings had barely made the playoffs.

But speedy Vikings wide receiver Anthony Carter had the game of his life against the 49ers, outplaying Rice in the process. Carter caught 10 passes for an incredible 227 yards to lead Minnesota to a victory.

The Vikings lost the NFC title game to Washington the following week. But they will forever be remembered as the team that manhandled Montana and the 49ers.

Anthony Carter made a phenomenal catch in the air during his amazing game against the 49ers.

NINERS GO YOUNG

Montana was benched in favor of Steve Young in the second half of the game. But Montana still had great years in front of him. He led the 49ers to two more Super Bowl victories.

FINAL SCORE

VIKINGS **36** | 49ERS **24**

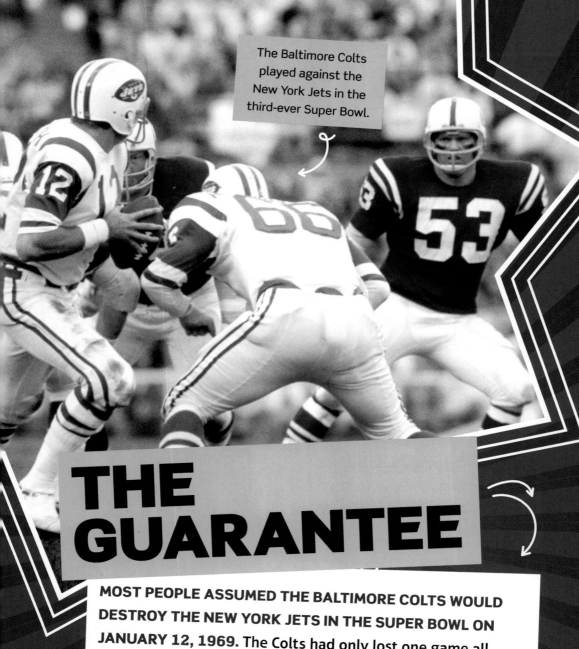

The Baltimore Colts played against the New York Jets in the third-ever Super Bowl.

THE GUARANTEE

MOST PEOPLE ASSUMED THE BALTIMORE COLTS WOULD DESTROY THE NEW YORK JETS IN THE SUPER BOWL ON JANUARY 12, 1969. The Colts had only lost one game all season in the NFL, which was considered by far to be the top league in the country. The Jets had won the AFL championship. But few believed the AFL was as **competitive** as the NFL. Baltimore was expected to win by at least three touchdowns.

One player believed New York would win and was bold enough to say it. That was Jets quarterback Joe Namath. He spoke up on the Thursday before the big game. He did not just predict a victory. He **guaranteed** it!

Many people just laughed at Namath. But they weren't laughing on Super Bowl Sunday. Matt Snell made it clear in the second quarter that the Jets were no pushovers. The big running back took a handoff from Namath and rolled left. He broke a tackle and dived into the end zone for the score.

Joe Namath played for the New York Jets from 1965 to 1976.

Jim Turner (*11*) made all three of his field goals for the Jets in the second half of Super Bowl III.

That was the only touchdown the Jets needed. Kicker Jim Turner did the rest. He booted three field goals to give his team a 16–0 lead. The Jets defense wrapped things up, shutting out Baltimore for three quarters and intercepting four passes.

Namath had made good on his promise. The Jets had pulled off one of the most incredible upsets of all time.

More than 75,000 people attended Super Bowl III. Jets fans were full of joy when their team pulled off the historic upset.

BIG CHANGES

The AFL and NFL merged in 1970 to form one league. In the "new" NFL, the AFL teams played in the American Football Conference (AFC). Three NFL teams joined them. The rest formed the NFC.

FINAL SCORE

JETS	COLTS
16	**7**

SEAHAWKS STUN SAINTS

THE 2010 SEATTLE SEAHAWKS MADE THE PLAYOFFS BY WINNING THEIR DIVISION WITH A WEAK 7-9 RECORD. Few thought they would beat the New Orleans Saints in the first round.

The Seattle Seahawks had the worst record of any team to reach the playoffs after the 2010 season. A win against the high-scoring Saints seemed unlikely.

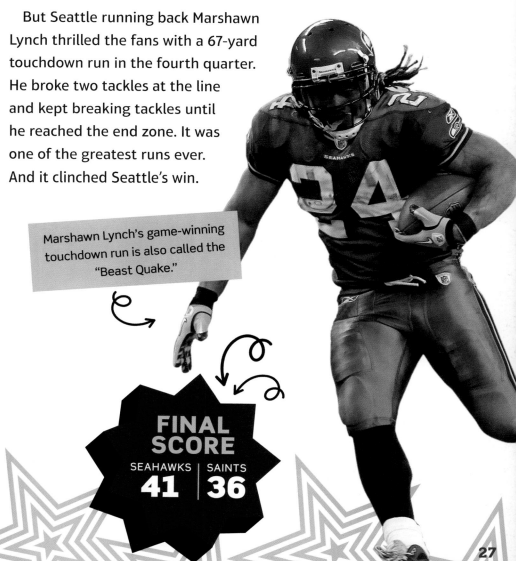

So it was no surprise when the Saints jumped ahead 17–7. But Seattle quarterback Matt Hasselbeck threw two touchdown passes in the second quarter and another early in the third.

New Orleans pushed back with back-to-back scoring drives. The Saints were only one touchdown away from retaking the lead.

But Seattle running back Marshawn Lynch thrilled the fans with a 67-yard touchdown run in the fourth quarter. He broke two tackles at the line and kept breaking tackles until he reached the end zone. It was one of the greatest runs ever. And it clinched Seattle's win.

Marshawn Lynch's game-winning touchdown run is also called the "Beast Quake."

FINAL SCORE

SEAHAWKS | SAINTS
41 | 36

OVERTIME

EVERY PLAYOFF TEAM HAS SOME GREAT PLAYERS. The best rise to the occasion with a championship on the line. It might be a quarterback or a wide receiver. It might be a linebacker or defensive back. The greatest perform the best when needed the most.

NFL players can't help but celebrate when their underdog team pulls ahead and wins.

Any NFL team can win on game day.

Major upsets have made the NFL exciting for nearly a century. **Expansion** has resulted in more teams playing in the league and more teams reaching the playoffs. And that means more chances for a big upset. These surprises help make professional football the most popular sport in the United States.

GLOSSARY

competitive: wanting to succeed in something

disbanded: no longer active or in existence

expansion: the process of adding teams to a league

fumbles: when players lose possession of a football and it is recovered by a teammate or the opposing team

guaranteed: predicted as sure to happen

interceptions: passes caught by players on the opposing team

underdog: team expected to lose a game

FURTHER INFORMATION

Christopher, Matt. *On the Field with … Tom Brady*. New York: Little, Brown, and Company, 2018.

Editors of Sports Illustrated Kids. *The Greatest Football Teams of All Time*. New York: Time Inc. Books, 2018.

Gary Gramling. *1st and 10: Top 10 Lists of Everything in Football*. New York: Liberty Street, 2016.

NFL.com
https://www.nfl.com

NFL Flag Football
https://nflflag.com

Sports Illustrated Kids: Football
https://www.sikids.com/football

INDEX

PHOTO ACKNOWLEDGMENTS

The images in this book are used with the permission of: © Brett Carlsen/Getty Images Sport/Getty Images, p. 4; © Michael Zagaris/Getty Images Sport/Getty Images, p. 6; © The Sporting News/Getty Images, p. 7; © New York Daily News Archive/New York Daily News/Getty Images, p. 8; © Andy Lyons/Getty Images Sport/Getty Images, p. 9; © Bettmann/Getty Images, pp. 10, 11, 18; © NFL Photos/AP Images, pp. 12, 13, 24; © Jamie Squire/Getty Images Sport/Getty Images, p. 14; © Otto Greule Jr/Getty Images Sport/Getty Images, pp. 15, 26, 29; © Focus On Sport/Getty Images Sport/Getty Images, pp. 16, 17, 23, 25; © Malcolm W. Emmons/Sporting News/Getty Images, p. 19; © Arthur Anderson/Getty Images Sport/Getty Images, pp. 20, 21; © Kidwiler Collection/Diamond Images/Getty Images, p. 22; © Jonathan Ferrey/Getty Images Sport/Getty Images, p. 27; © Stephen Maturen/Getty Images Sport/Getty Images, p. 28.

Front cover: © Focus on Sport/Getty Images Sport/Getty Images, top left, bottom; © Gary W. Green/MCT/Tribune News Service/Getty Images, top right.